BITTER OR
BETTER

Emerging Victorious
through Trials

DON SISK

First published in 2010 by Striving Together Publications, a
ministry of Lancaster Baptist Church, Lancaster, CA 93535.
Striving Together Publications is committed to providing
tried, trusted, and proven books that will further equip local
churches to carry out the Great Commission. Your comments
and suggestions are valued.

Striving Together Publications
4020 E. Lancaster Blvd.
Lancaster, CA 93535
800.201.7748
www.strivingtogether.com

Cover design by Andrew Jones
Layout by Craig Parker
Edited by Ashlee Dickerson and Monica Bass
Special thanks to our proofreaders

ISBN 978-1-59894-109-8

Printed in the United States of America

Contents

Introduction

The world is full of hurting people—families torn apart by broken promises, children abused by should-be protectors, employees smarting under unfair accusations, lonely people missing their loved ones. Perhaps you picked up this book because you are hurting; you could add your own suffering to the list above.

The pain inflicted on us has a way of changing us—shaping our outlook and controlling our responses. Too often the end of trials is anger, resentment, and bitterness. But God has a better way. He can take the darkest circumstances and turn them into the brightest joys for those who allow Him to do so. Our natural response to suffering is to become bitter, but God desires to use that very suffering to make us better.

Evangelist Charles Weigle was well acquainted with the bitter dregs of grief. One evening he returned home after a revival meeting and found a note from his wife. "Charlie," she wrote, "I've been a fool. I've done without a lot of things long enough." She wrote a few more lines expressing her frustration of living the life of an evangelist's wife and finished, "for me— it's goodbye."

Reeling from the pain of his wife's desertion, Charles sank into a deep depression. For several years, he allowed despair to control his life and at times even contemplated suicide. In his intense misery, he wondered if anyone ever truly cared for him at all.

By God's grace, Charles eventually remembered Who did care for him with infinite tenderness. He stopped allowing the devil to whisper thoughts of despair and hopelessness, and, with his faith restored, he penned the words to one of the most comforting hymns ever written:

I would love to tell you what I think of Jesus,
Since I found in Him a friend so strong and true;
I would tell you how He changed my life completely,
He did something that no other friend could do.

No one ever cared for me like Jesus,
There's no other friend so kind as He;
No one else could take the sin and darkness from me,
O how much He cared for me.

All my life was full of sin when Jesus found me,
All my heart was full of misery and woe;
Jesus placed His strong and loving arms about me,
And He led me in the way I ought to go.

Ev'ry day He comes to me with new assurance,
More and more I understand His words of love;
But I'll never know just why He came to save me,
Till some day I see His blessed face above.

Charles learned that as long as he allowed himself to wallow in self-pity and bitterness, he was miserable and ineffective for Christ. But once he chose to remember God's goodness, care, and faithfulness, God used him through song to help countless others experiencing similar trials.

When experiencing heartache, we are faced with a choice—a choice many of us never consider. Like Charles Weigle, we can either become bitter or better as a result of the pain in our lives.

Hebrews 12:15 warns us against bitterness: *"lest any root of bitterness springing up trouble you, and thereby many be defiled."* If you allow trials to make you bitter, you limit your effectiveness for God. Ephesians 4:31 instructs, *"Let all bitterness...be put away from you...."*

But is it possible to eliminate anger and bitterness and find joy in the midst of pain? In Philippians 4:4, Paul instructed, *"Rejoice in the Lord alway: and again I say, Rejoice."* This may seem like a trite, even insensitive, statement until one remembers that Paul wrote these words from prison. Paul learned what we will discover in these pages—that God is bigger than any difficulty we face, and when we look to Him and trust in His goodness, we will always have reason for rejoicing.

In this book, we will examine why God allows heartaches into our lives and how our response to them determines our future usefulness. We'll explore four truths that can make the difference in our trials. Fully embracing these truths steers us from the path of bitterness and allows God to use our trials to make us better instead.

CHAPTER ONE

God Is in Control of Our Circumstances

Some truths are easy to believe, and even to teach, when they are least needed. That God is in control over our circumstances is one such truth. When circumstantial sunshine is bright in my life, it is a joy to remember that God is in control. But when dark storm clouds gather and the howling wind whistles with fear, it is then I most need to believe that God truly is in control. For it is during such perilous times that faith in God's promises provides a refuge from the fiercest effects of the storm.

Romans 8:28 promises, *"And we know that all things work together for good to them that love God, to them who are the called according to his purpose."* Every trial you encounter may not seem good. In fact, none of them do—at first. Only God could make good on such a promise.

So, how can this be possible? How can all things work together for good?

Viewing Romans 8:28 in its larger context enables us to better understand the good that God guarantees through trials. Verse 29 continues, *"For whom he did foreknow, he also did predestinate to be conformed to the image of his Son, that he might be the firstborn among many brethren."* Before you can see God's purpose in trials, you must understand that whatever He is allowing in your life, He is using as a tool to achieve His ultimate goal of conforming you to the image of Jesus Christ.

Although God loves you and wants you to live joyfully in Him, He is more concerned in your being conformed to the image of Christ than with your immediate comfort. He is more interested in your holiness than your happiness. When a trial enters your life, it is imperative that you understand that God allowed the trial in order to shape and mold you into the image of His Son.

When trials come our way, we tend to focus on how we will get through them. We worry, fret, and despair. However, when we remember that God is in control, we can turn our focus to why He allows trials—to conform us to His own image. Rather than looking for an escape, we should keep in mind that God will work everything out for good.

First Peter 2:9–10 gives a unique picture of God taking care of His children: *"But ye are a chosen generation, a royal priesthood, an holy nation, a peculiar people; that ye should shew forth the praises of him who hath called you out of darkness into his marvellous light: Which in time past were not a people, but are now the people of God: which had not obtained mercy, but now have obtained mercy."*

The word *peculiar* in this passage comes from the Greek word *peripoiesis*, which refers to possessions or personal property. It is comprised of the preposition *peri*, "around or encircled," and the noun *poiesis*, "something that is made or done." Greek scholar Kenneth Wuest says *peripoiesis* "means literally 'to make around,' that is, to make something and then to surround it with a circle, thus indicating ownership."

As sinners saved by grace, we who were at one time alienated and separated from God are now His peculiar people—we are literally encircled by Him.

Nothing can reach us as a child of God, except it pass through the Father's hand: *"My sheep hear my voice, and I know them, and they follow me: And I give unto them eternal life; and they shall never perish, neither shall any man pluck them out of my hand. My Father, which gave them me, is greater than all; and no man is able to pluck them out of my Father's hand"* (John 10:27–29).

What a wonderful position we have as believers! We are in the hand of the Lord Jesus Christ, and His hand is in the hand of God the Father. Any circumstance that comes our way must either come from God or through God. This position does not protect us from all trials, but it does ensure that the trials permitted to enter our lives are all "Father-filtered." God will only allow that which He knows can ultimately conform us to the image of Christ.

The life of Job illustrates God's sovereignty over our circumstances. Job chapter 1 records the tremendous losses Job experienced: loss of his flocks, his herds, his home, his health, his friends, and most grievous of all, his children. Yet, we see unmistakably in God's Word that every loss Job encountered was first permitted by God. Satan literally had to ask God's permission before he could touch Job's possessions, family, or health. Although God allowed these trials, He restricted Satan from taking Job's life.

In the midst of tragedy, we witness Job choosing to trust God. With a trust foreign to most Christians, he cried, *"Though he slay me, yet will I trust in him…"* (Job 13:15). Although Job couldn't understand God's purposes in what He allowed, he determined to trust.

The final chapter in Job's life records God's goodness. The Lord restored all of Job's wealth—in double—and gave him ten more children. Everything worked together for good.

To be sure, the devil is a roaring lion who would love to devour us (1 Peter 5:8). But, thank God, this lion is on a leash! Not only does our Heavenly Father limit Satan's ability to harm, but He unfailingly holds us in the security of His hand.

Circumstances thus filtered by God can never destroy us, but our responses can. When we doubt God's goodness and resist His Spirit's work to conform us to Christ, we become bitter and disillusioned. But when we trust God's promises, love Him, and yield to His purposes, we will experience the good that God intends to bring through trials. God alone, the Creator and Sustainer of the universe, has the power to work everything together for good.

CHAPTER TWO

God Will Avenge His People

Some trials have a definite conclusion—most financial trials, for example. When God provides the funds, the trial is over, and it is easy to see in hindsight that God worked everything for good. Other trials are not so neatly tucked behind us—some situations affect the very core of our emotions.

When facing trials caused by others, our minds may know that God will work everything together for good, but there is a hurting and wounded heart deep within that is not often readily convinced. Perhaps everyone around assumes that our pain has passed with the passing of our circumstances, but we may be suffering from a bitter and vengeful heart raging within us.

God has a wonderful answer to our need for vengeance: entrust it to Him. God sees every wrong done to you, and you can trust Him to make it right. *"...Vengeance is mine; I will repay, saith the Lord"* (Romans 12:19).

Somehow, we believe that remaining angry and bitter protects us from the pain inflicted on us and will allow us to properly settle the accounts. In reality, holding on to the need to execute justice towards those who have hurt you only fills your own heart with bitterness. As it has been said, bitterness hurts more the vessel in which it is stored than the vessel on which it is poured. The person who suffers most from bitterness is the one who harbors it.

Unlike God, who chooses to *"remember no more"* our sins against Him (Hebrews 10:17), our flesh revels in sustaining an elephant-like memory! Forgiveness is not a natural response. Forgiveness is a choice we must make and the only way to reclaim joy.

> *Bless them which persecute you: bless, and curse not.*
> *Rejoice with them that do rejoice, and weep with*
> *them that weep. Be of the same mind one toward*

another. Mind not high things, but condescend to men of low estate: Be not wise in your own conceits. Recompense to no man evil for evil. Provide things honest in the sight of all men. If it be possible, as much as lieth in you, live peaceably with all men. Dearly beloved, avenge not yourselves, but rather give place unto wrath: for it is written, Vengeance is mine; I will repay, saith the Lord. Therefore if thine enemy hunger, feed him; if he thirst, give him drink: for in so doing thou shalt heap coals of fire on his head. Be not overcome of evil, but overcome evil with good.—ROMANS 12:14–21

When we repay the evil done to us with good, God promises to take care of retribution. God will avenge His people; we can leave vengeance with Him.

In a world full of sinners and imperfect saints, you will undoubtedly meet someone you are unable to live with peaceably—even when you are doing your best to repay good for evil. For this reason, Scripture specifies **"*If it be possible*, *as much as lieth in you, live peaceably with all men…avenge not yourselves…*"** [emphasis added]. When you are confronted with impossible people, do all you can to live in peace with them, but when it just doesn't work, do not seek revenge for the wrong they do to you.

Years ago, the Lord convicted me that I should leave the Baptist denomination I was a part of and become an Independent Baptist. Today there are many reasons I am thankful I followed the Lord's direction in this, but at the time, it was very difficult. Men with whom I had enjoyed Christian fellowship misinterpreted my actions and misrepresented my motives. Some hurled hurtful words and told others I was no longer a Baptist at all.

In fleshly anger, I began making plans to confront these men. But God spoke to my heart through Romans 12:14–21. He taught me that it's not up to me to avenge myself, but rather, vengeance is His jurisdiction. My Father knows what injustices come into my life, and He promises to deal with them personally. He taught me a great lesson in those painful circumstances as He enabled me to trust Him for vengeance and forgive my offenders.

Abraham posed a fitting question in Genesis 18:25: "...*Shall not the Judge of all the earth do right?*" We can answer with a resounding, "Yes!" God will make everything right—in His time.

Meanwhile, even through the pain inflicted by others, God desires to conform us to the image of Christ "*Who, when he was reviled, reviled not again;*

when he suffered, he threatened not; but committed himself to him that judgeth righteously" (1 Peter 2:23). The only right choice—the healing and cleansing choice for the Christian—is to reject bitterness and allow God to use the pain inflicted by others to make us more like Jesus.

CHAPTER THREE

God's People Are Often Treated Unfairly

Scripture abounds with examples of God's people who were treated unfairly. These saints endured hardness, choosing to become better through their trials.

Joseph

Joseph was sold into slavery by his brothers, lied about by an adulterous woman, and thrown into an Egyptian prison. Despite everything he endured, not once did he complain against God. He chose instead to forgive. (We will look at the life of Joseph in more detail later.)

Stephen

Stephen became the first martyr of the church—
stoned simply for preaching the Gospel. Even as the
stones were striking his body, Stephen *"kneeled down,
and cried with a loud voice, Lord, lay not this sin to
their charge..."* (Acts 7:60). Instead of becoming bitter
toward those who were taking his life, Stephen asked
God to forgive them! If only more Christians would
forgive so selflessly the minor offences committed
against them.

Paul

Paul was a witness to the death of Stephen, and it
had a profound impact on his life. Other than Jesus
Christ, Paul became perhaps the greatest preacher of
the Gospel the world has ever seen. But Paul endured
an amazing amount of suffering: stoning, multiple
shipwrecks, imprisonment, and eventual martyrdom.
Yet in 2 Corinthians 4:17, he referred to his trials as
"light affliction"! How could he say that being stoned
was a light affliction? Paul viewed his earthly pain
in light of heavenly rewards, and he compared his
temporary discomforts to what they would produce in
eternal joys.

Jesus Christ

The ultimate example of one who received unfair treatment is Jesus Christ. From birth to His ascension, He never once sinned; He was the impeccable Son of God. Yet even in the presence of perfection, men falsely accused Christ. He was called the devil by religious hypocrites, beaten beyond recognition by Roman soldiers, and nailed to a cross with a crown of thorns on His head. (It's humbling to realize that Christ willingly endured this torment because of His love for us.) In excruciating pain, Jesus called upon His Father to forgive His persecutors: *"Then said Jesus, Father, forgive them; for they know not what they do..."* (Luke 23:34). No doubt, it is from Christ's example that Stephen learned how to forgive.

You

You can fill in your story here—someone has embarrassed you, accused you, abused you, or treated you unfairly. The pain others inflict can wound deeply. Hopefully after reading the stories of these men of God, including His Son, you will find comfort in knowing that you are not the only one enduring suffering.

Even as the men listed above triumphed in the midst of suffering, the story of your suffering doesn't have to end in bitterness and defeat. God promises blessing to those who are persecuted for His sake:

> *Blessed are they which are persecuted for righteousness' sake: for theirs is the kingdom of heaven. Blessed are ye, when men shall revile you, and persecute you, and shall say all manner of evil against you falsely, for my sake. Rejoice, and be exceeding glad: for great is your reward in heaven: for so persecuted they the prophets which were before you.—*MATTHEW 5:10–12

Second Timothy 3:12 tells us that if we are living righteously, we can count on encountering persecution: *"Yea, and all that will live godly in Christ Jesus shall suffer persecution."* If you never endure persecution for Christ, it could be an indication that you are not right with God. Of course, this does not mean that the only people who are truly right with God are those who are suffering at this moment for righteousness' sake, and it certainly does not mean that everyone who is suffering is right with God. There is a difference between persecution and chastisement.

Chastisement is God's correction for disobedient children. When His children follow the fleshly impulses of their own wills, He lovingly, but firmly chastises them to turn their hearts back toward Himself. Before claiming God's promises of blessing in persecution, you should determine if the cause of your trial is actually God's chastisement for sin in your life. Ask the Lord to bring to mind any unconfessed sin that could be prompting His correction. Rest assured that if God is chastening you, He will show you the reason when you ask Him.

When your Heavenly Father reveals sin, make it right immediately by confessing it to Him and turning your heart and ways back to His commands. Proverbs 28:13 says, *"He that covereth his sins shall not prosper: but whoso confesseth and forsaketh them shall have mercy."* First John 1:9 further promises, *"If we confess our sins, he is faithful and just to forgive us our sins, and to cleanse us from all unrighteousness."*

When persecution "for righteousness' sake," enters your life, God has special instructions for you:

> *Beloved, think it not strange concerning the fiery trial which is to try you, as though some strange thing happened unto you: But rejoice, inasmuch*

*as ye are partakers of Christ's sufferings; that,
when his glory shall be revealed, ye may be glad
also with exceeding joy. If ye be reproached for
the name of Christ, happy are ye; for the spirit of
glory and of God resteth upon you: on their part
he is evil spoken of, but on your part he is glorified.*
—1 PETER 4:12–14

Don't be surprised when you are mistreated.
Rejoice! You have an opportunity to share in the Lord's
sufferings and bear reproach for His name.

There are many who would have us believe
a "prosperity gospel"—that after salvation, all of
our problems disappear. Yet God's Word and the
testimonies of God's servants indicates just the
opposite. After salvation, you will actually have more
problems than you had before, as you will now, at
times, suffer for Christ.

Don't become disheartened. God's people have
often been treated unfairly, but God always balances
the scales. He is in control of every circumstance in our
lives, and He will make everything right in the end.

Psalm 34:19 says, *"Many are the afflictions of the
righteous: but the LORD delivereth him out of them all."*
Although God did not promise a smooth journey, He
did promise to provide all the comfort, grace, and

strength we need along the way. He leads us toward a final destination of joy that far surpasses any pain we endure here. Let God work everything in your life for good.

CHAPTER FOUR

God Determines Your Usefulness by Your Responses

I t's not hard to understand that trials will come—that's just part of life. But it is difficult to consistently respond with the grace of God and to practice forgiveness toward those who have hurt you.

The determining factor in the result of our trials is not the circumstances themselves but our reactions to them. If you retaliate to mistreatment, you give up control of yourself by allowing the hurt to dictate your reaction. Instead, allow responses to be controlled by God. Follow Christ's instructions in Matthew 5:44 to "...*Love your enemies, bless them that curse you, do good to them that hate you, and pray for them which despitefully use you, and persecute you.*" Because any circumstances that come your way are filtered through your Heavenly Father's hand, nothing anybody can do to you has the power to ultimately harm you. It can, and often does, hurt you, but only your reaction can harm you. It is your response, not others' actions, that determine your usefulness to God.

Just as a tea bag submerged in hot water reveals its flavor, so your response to adversity demonstrates your true character. The goal for all of us is that our responses would mirror the character of Christ that God is developing through trials.

Let's examine the lives of two men who both encountered severe difficulties with two very different ends. Notice how their responses determined if they would become bitter or better.

Ahithophel became bitter.

The wisest counselor in King David's cabinet was a man by the name of Ahithophel. Second Samuel 16:23 tells us that Ahithophel's counsel was *"as if a man had enquired at the oracle of God."* This man was very close to David—a dear friend.

Yet, when David's son Absalom led a national rebellion against his father, Ahithophel sided with Absalom and counseled the would-be king in the best way to kill David and secure the kingdom. Ahithophel even volunteered to do the favor himself: *"Moreover Ahithophel said unto Absalom, Let me now choose out twelve thousand men, and I will arise and pursue after David this night: And I will come upon him while he is weary and weak handed, and will make him afraid: and all the people that are with him shall flee; and I will smite the king only"* (2 Samuel 17:1–2).

What happened to the friendship between David and Ahithophel? Where did it go wrong? What could have so embittered Ahithophel that he would actually plot David's destruction?

A few chapters back in 2 Samuel 11, we find the tragic and sordid account of King David's adulterous relationship with Bathsheba. The genealogical record in the following verses shed light on Ahithophel's bitterness toward David:

Eliphelet the son of Ahasbai, the son of the Maachathite, **Eliam the son of Ahithophel** *the Gilonite.*—2 SAMUEL 23:34 [emphasis added]

> *And David sent and enquired after the woman.*
> *And one said, Is not this* **Bathsheba, the**
> **daughter of Eliam,** *the wife of Uriah the Hittite?*
> —2 Samuel 11:3 [emphasis added]

Ahithophel's son was named Eliam, and Eliam was the father of Bathsheba, making Ahithophel Bathsheba's grandfather. When David committed adultery with Bathsheba, he did so knowing that she was the granddaughter of his dear friend and counselor Ahithophel, yet in David's lust, he disregarded his relationship with Ahithophel. To make matters worse, David then had Bathsheba's husband Uriah killed in a botched attempt to cover his sin. In base selfishness, he tried to protect his own reputation while violating Ahithophel's family in the worst way.

Ahithophel allowed this bitterness to seethe in his heart for many years. When Absalom rebelled, Ahithophel seized his opportunity for revenge and counseled Absalom in his own murderous plot.

If Absalom had heeded Ahithophel's advice, David would indeed have been killed. However, by God's grace Absalom rejected Ahithophel's counsel, opting instead for another plan to take the kingdom, and God used this overturned counsel to spare David's life.

This final rejection was too much for Ahithophel to handle, and 2 Samuel 17:23 reveals the tragic result of his bitterness: *"And when Ahithophel saw that his counsel was not followed, he saddled his ass, and arose, and gat him home to his house, to his city, and put his household in order, and hanged himself, and died, and was buried in the sepulchre of his father."*

Ahithophel allowed bitterness to control, and eventually end, his life. David's sin against Ahithophel and his family was indeed great (and God thoroughly chastened David for it), but Ahithophel's reaction brought even greater consequences to himself. The target of Ahithophel's bitterness was David, but whose life suffered more from this bitterness—David's or Ahithophel's?

Let Ahithophel's life serve as a reminder that bitterness against another will ultimately harm your own life. You may not respond with the murderous rage of Ahithophel, but any level of bitterness will have the same result—self-destruction.

Joseph became better.

Joseph's journey from a pit to a prison to a palace is extraordinary. Because we are already familiar with the end of this story, it's easy for us to see that God was working in every ordeal Joseph endured along the way. For Joseph, however, the journey was treacherous, lined with untold opportunities to detour toward bitterness. It seemed that every time Joseph resisted temptation, circumstances simply became worse. And it seemed that every time things were starting to go right, his life was turned upside down all over again.

As with Job, each trial in Joseph's life was allowed by God. From his brothers selling him into slavery, to Potiphar's wife's false accusations, to his banishment into prison, to his being forgotten by the one person who could help him out of prison—God made it all work for good. God used every situation that Joseph went through to bring him to the place where he could accomplish God's will for his life.

If Joseph's brothers had not sold him into slavery, Joseph would never have worked for Potiphar. If Potiphar's wife had not accused Joseph wrongly, he would never have spent time in the king's prison. If Joseph had not been in that particular prison, he never would have met Pharaoh's butler and interpreted his dream. If Joseph had not accurately interpreted the butler's dream, the butler would have never suggested that Joseph interpret Pharaoh's dream. If Joseph had not interpreted Pharaoh's dream, no one would have known to save provisions for the coming years of famine, and Joseph certainly would not have become the prime minister of Egypt. God used all these events to put Joseph in the right place at the right time to save his family from starvation.

Years earlier, Joseph's jealous brothers could never have guessed that by seemingly destroying Joseph's life, they were actually participating in God's plan for their own salvation and the salvation of countless others. (Doesn't this sound similar to Christ's sacrifice on the Cross? The very people responsible for nailing Jesus to the Cross had no idea that they were participating in paving the way for eternal salvation.)

Throughout Joseph's entire journey, the Lord was with him; four times in Genesis 39 Scripture records this fact (Genesis 39:2–3, 21, 23). Rather than becoming bitter toward those who wronged him, Joseph chose to remember God's faithfulness and trust that God had a purpose for his life.

The main emphasis of this story is that Joseph remained faithful. For this reason, he rose to prominence in every position—Potiphar's house, the prison, and even the palace. It was faithfulness that positioned Joseph to experience God's blessings.

The greatest revelation of Joseph's character came after his father's death. Fearful of receiving well-deserved revenge, Joseph's brothers fell before him and plead his forgiveness. However, their guilty consciences had nothing to fear, for Joseph had truly forgiven his brothers long before he knew that he would ever see them again.

We see Joseph's heart of forgiveness in the name he chose for his first son: "*And unto Joseph were born two sons before the years of famine came, which Asenath the daughter of Potipherah priest of On bare unto him. And Joseph called the name of the firstborn Manasseh: For God, said he, hath made me forget all my toil, and all my father's house*" (Genesis 41:50–51). Joseph chose to trust his painful past to God and remain faithful in whatever place God allowed him to serve.

Although Joseph now had the power to accomplish his own revenge against his brothers, he knew it was not his place. Instead, he answered his brothers' anxious pleas with words of forgiveness and faith: "*And Joseph said unto them, Fear not: for am I in the place of God? But as for you, ye thought evil against me; but God meant it unto good, to bring to pass, as it is this day, to save much people alive. Now therefore fear ye not: I will nourish you, and your little ones.*

And he comforted them, and spake kindly unto them" (Genesis 50:19–21).

Because Joseph chose to trust God rather than to become bitter, God turned the wicked plots of dark-hearted men to bring about the deliverance of Joseph's entire family as well as the nation of Egypt in time of famine.

But what if Joseph had chosen bitterness? He would never have become the second-highest man in Egypt, countless lives would have been lost in the famine (including his own and his family's), and he would never have seen his father again. If Joseph had become bitter, he would have endured all the trials but never known the good God could have brought out of such impossible situations.

Ahithophel and Joseph—what opposite responses! Ahithophel compounded his suffering by bitterness. By seeking revenge, he missed out on the good that God brought through tragedy. His great-grandson, who later became King Solomon, would never know him, and he missed the opportunity to be a godly example for Solomon.

Joseph trusted God with the larger picture. Being torn away from his father and getting thrown into prison was not what he would have planned for his life, but he recognized God's hand in every circumstance, and entire nations were blessed because of his faith.

No one is exempt from trials. Some circumstances have no way of escape and no option for control. What we can control, however, is our responses. May we learn from the lives of Ahithophel and Joseph to reject bitterness and embrace forgiveness. The God of Joseph is our God, and He can turn the worst experiences into the greatest blessings—in our own lives and in the lives of others.

CONCLUSION

I don't know what trials you may be experiencing that prompted you to pick up this book, but I do know the God who allowed the trials to enter into your life. And because I know Him and have experienced His faithfulness and trust His promises, I know that He can use whatever you are dealing with for your good.

God is working something far bigger than you or anyone else can imagine. If you will cling to Him in faith and press onward even when you don't understand, God will make all things work together for good in *your* life.

"...*Shall not the Judge of all the earth do right?*" (Genesis 18:25). Of course He will. God may not judge the work of man instantly as we would like Him to, but He does make everything right in the end.

We can't control the circumstances life hurls our way. But we can choose our responses to life's ups and downs.

God has an incredible destination for your life's journey. When your path becomes difficult and painful, you can either detour to the easier trail of bitterness and miss participating in the miracles God will do in your life, or you can persevere in joyful trust and watch God's plan unfold. It's your decision: will you become bitter or better?

"*And we know that all things work together for good to them that love God, to them who are the called according to his purpose*" (Romans 8:28).

Visit us online

strivingtogether.com

wcbc.edu